God Bless My
Senior
Moments

Karen O'Connor

HARVEST HOUSE PUBLISHERS
EUGENE, OREGON

Cover illustration © Cedric Hohnstadt

Cover design by Dugan Design Group, Bloomington, Minnesota.

Published in association with the Books & Such Literary Agency, 52 Mission Circle, Suite 122, PMB 170, Santa Rosa, CA 95409-5370, www.booksandsuch.biz.

GOD BLESS MY SENIOR MOMENTS
Copyright © 2014 by Karen O'Connor
Published by Harvest House Publishers
Eugene, Oregon 97408
www.harvesthousepublishers.com

ISBN 978-0-7369-5382-5 (pbk.)
ISBN 978-0-7369-5383-2 (eBook)

Printed in the United States of America

19 20 21 22 / BP-JC / 20 19 18

To Charles,
my husband and
prayer partner

To all seniors like me. God does bless us!

God Smiles with Us

After writing *365 Reasons Why Gettin' Old Ain't So Bad* and *365 Senior Moments You'd Rather Forget*, I got to thinking about the importance of prayer at this stage of life. It's fun to laugh at our foibles and follies. We seniors need a chuckle as much as anyone, especially when we forget where we put our glasses (on our heads) and misplace our written prescriptions (we use the backs to write grocery lists). But we also need to pray and be prayed for—at least I do.

To that end, I've combined humor and prayer in this book. I trust God is smiling right along with us as we stumble into those awkward moments that are common to all of us as we grow older, wiser, and more real regarding how we look and what we say. It's okay to make a mistake or to misstep. We're only human, after all. There are also plenty of tender and sweet moments to celebrate during our senior years!

I hope you enjoy reading and talking to God as you use the short prayers in this book. If they encourage you to share some of your own humorous experiences and prayers, that's great too. And if you'd like to send them along to me, feel free to email them to *karen@karenoconnor.com*. Perhaps they'll be included in my next book! Supporting each other through laughter and prayer are the best ways we can help each other during this season of life.

May God bless you, look after you when senior moments hit, and bring joy to all your relationships.

Karen O'Connor
Watsonville, California

Lord, what a relief to focus on what you think of me instead of what other people think. May I always keep my eyes on you.

Dear God, I chuckle when I think of my stubborn streak. Sometimes I cling to being right even when I'm wrong—like today when my husband told me the bug I was chasing wasn't there. It was simply a floater in my eye.

Lord, thank you for keeping me sane this morning when I dropped my blouse into the trash compactor and scraped my leftover cereal into the clothes hamper.

O God, I'm so grateful to know that as I lay my head on my pillow at night, I have your assurance that when the alarm clock rings tomorrow morning, I'll get to it without falling out of bed.

Thank you, heavenly Father, that in these later years I can take a nap if I wish and not feel guilty for giving myself some time to rest.

O Lord, how much I love the little things in life—including the tweet of a bird, the fragrance of a flower, and the sound of a baby laughing.

What a joy, dear God, to relax with my husband in the same room without saying a word to each other. We're as comfy and familiar with each other as a pair of well-worn, best-loved slippers.

Whew! Thank you, Lord, for helping us get out of debt—financially and in relationships.

God, it's a good thing you reminded me to turn on the stove or our oatmeal would taste more like watery soup than hot cereal.

Instant coffee or ground flax? That was close. If I hadn't paused to read the label, I'd have used the wrong jar. Thank you, God, for telling me to slow down before it was too late.

Good catch, Lord! You flagged me before I inserted my Target card into the ATM slot.

Thank you, Lord, for reminding me to pick up the book I just bought to help me with memory loss.

I'm grateful, God, that you're watching out for me when I'm not. You helped me get through the list of introductions at our homeowners party without missing a beat. I wish I'd asked you to help me remember my husband's name though…

Lord, my new hairstyle is on account of you. I lost the photo of the style I wanted so I got this one instead. Thanks for leading the way. I like it.

How embarrassing, God. I called someone I know well and then forgot her name when she answered the phone. I'm glad you know the names of all my friends so you could bail me out by bringing it to my mind.

Oh no, dear God, another check went into the mail before I signed it. Please help me slow down and take one step at a time.

Lord, help me put first things first, such as waiting for the microwave timer to go off before leaving the room. Otherwise I'm likely to find a cup of cold tea in there tomorrow morning.

O Lord, what is with me? This morning I tried to crack an orange instead of an egg—until you tapped me on the shoulder. Thank you.

Thank you, God, for the stamina I needed to push the loaded supermarket cart from the store exit to my car. But what was I thinking after that? I opened the rear door of my car, dropped the cart off in the return area, and drove away. I left the groceries in the cart! Please let them still be there when I get back to the store.

Lord, I'm thankful for the eyes to see the child who darted in front of my car. Thank you for the ears to hear your reminder to slow down when I entered this neighborhood.

Heavenly Father, lead me in the way I need to go when it comes to hearing the pain and hurt in another person's life. Give me the wisdom and patience to listen instead of barreling ahead with my woes.

My purpose is to give life in all its fullness" (John 10:10). Lord, what a comfort you are.

Jesus, be with me, please, especially when I stumble over a word or trip on a step. Pick me up, dust me off, and encourage me so I'm ready to go again.

Lord, I have bills to pay today. Please gently coach me to make sure I put the correct checks in the appropriate envelopes.

Oops! Lord, I need help cleaning out the clutter in my desk drawers. I tend to hang on to stuff I no longer need. Teach me to let go of the old and welcome the new.

Thank you, God, for keeping me from putting my new shoes in the giveaway box and keeping the old ones. I wonder where my mind is sometimes.

Lord, did I leave my cell phone in Donna's car? I hope not 'cause she's on vacation. Please help me find it.

Ah, thank you, God, for your quick response. I found my phone right where I must have put it—next to a box of strawberries in the fridge!

Good thinking, Lord! Thanks to you I remembered to take my mailbox key when I went to the post office.

Lord, that's it on writing reminder notes. I always lose them or forget to check them. Today I'm going to rely on your memory. I love you.

God, here's to my new stove! With your help, may I never start a kitchen fire or ruin a good cooking pot again because I forgot to turn off a burner.

I'm praising you today and every day, dear Lord, for your faithfulness to me even when I have a mental slip like I did today when I put the dog's toys in the crib with my grandson.

Lord, it's a good thing I'm forgetful sometimes. It helps me avoid sharing gossip about a friend or neighbor.

Lord, what's this I see in my knitting basket? A nutcracker instead of knitting needles? How did that happen? O God, please save me from myself.

Dear God, thank you that I'm now wise enough to put life in perspective. You've shown me how to enjoy each moment instead of lamenting my past mistakes and those annoying senior moments.

How happy I am, Lord, that when I goof up like I did today—running water through the garden hose until it flooded my flowerbed—you are here to rescue me.

Thanks, God, for bringing my best friend's name to mind right before she picked me up for our weekly luncheon.

Ta-da! Lord, thanks to you I found my car keys—in the ignition. Fortunately the car was still in the garage.

What a blessing, dear God, to lean on you even while I use a cane. You're the best and true security.

I'm so grateful that I snatched that coffee cup before it hit the floor. Thank you for helping me catch it just in the nick of time.

Whew! I actually remembered to butter my toast this morning instead of leaving it in the toaster until it turned hard and stale. Thank you, Lord, for keeping my mind active.

You saved me a big bill today, God. Thank you that the clicking sound in my car was simply the keys hitting each other as I drove.

O Lord, how foolish I am sometimes. Today I left my favorite book on a fence post when I went for a walk. I looked all over for it…until my neighbor found it and asked me if I'd lost it.

Father, I was pretty exasperated today when I tried to answer a phone call with the TV remote. Thank you for giving me a sense of humor so I can laugh at such silly mistakes.

Now, God, I must know. What is going on with me that I'd put my toothbrush in the dishwasher and leave the kitchen scrub brush in the bathroom? Am I losing my mind? If so, please rescue me!

Pills, pills, and more pills. If I took the advice dished out on TV, I'd be swallowing medicine at every meal. Help me, dear God, to rely on you as my medical guide.

How embarrassing, Father. I missed the symphony because I had the wrong date written on my calendar. Help me pay more attention to what I'm doing.

Ah, Lord, you caught me before I paid my utility bill twice and neglected to pay the phone bill. Once again, I thank you.

Dear God, I come to you embarrassed to admit I gargled with sugar instead of salt. Kinda sweet though, wouldn't you say?

Lord, I need a dose of sanity. I just put the cat's food in the birdcage and birdseed in Kitty's dish. Help!

This print looks a little blurred, Lord. Do I need new glasses so soon? Oops! These are my husband's specs! When will I get this straight?

God, please lend a hand here. I'm overwhelmed with holiday activities. I have 10 wrapped gifts on the counter, and I can't remember which one is which and for whom.

Lord, why do I try to save money by cutting my own hair? I did cut it, and now I have to pay someone to repair what I've done. Please give me your grace today.

Lord, I tried something new today. I put on two different earrings—but not on purpose. I never noticed until my granddaughter told me I looked cool. That made me smile.

Dear God, how did I mistake chicken stock for lemonade? Ugh. That's what I get for using the same color plastic pitchers for both.

I need to apologize to a friend, Lord, for giving her a ticket to a concert that had already occurred. Help me find the right words.

O God, how can I be surprised that onions popped up in my garden instead of tulips when the truth is I must have planted onion bulbs? A gardener I'm not!

Lord, you were there when I brushed my teeth with antibiotic cream and then later treated my cut with toothpaste. What's to become of me with such senior moments to distract me?

What's going on? I have the leash but where's the dog? Oh! At home by the front door probably—waiting for me to take him on a walk. Oh my. God, I do need your help today.

Father God, help me keep my cool now
that I realize I mailed a check without finishing the address on the front.
Thankfully, I remembered to put on
a return address sticker. Bring it back
quickly, please.

Lord, thank you for saving me a big
oops by reminding me to make sure my
shoes match before I walked out the
door.

Dear God, please tell my legs to cooper-
ate when I want to stand up and to bend
gently when I want to sit down.

I thank you and praise you, Lord, for showing me in the nick of time the difference between suntan lotion and sunscreen. I don't want to bake in the sun.

Lord, the mosquitoes swarmed around me when I used cologne instead of insect repellant on my arms and neck. What was I thinking of? Not much, apparently.

Dear God, when will I learn to prepare a meal so all the items finish at the same time? Does this mean my days in the kitchen are over? I hope not because I like my own cooking—even when I have to serve the items in courses as they get done.

O Lord, not again! I shredded a check and saved the envelope, and then I cut up the new credit card and saved the one that expired. I really need your comfort right now.

God, please help me remember my adult children's names when I introduce them to my friends. Also help me recall the names of my friends when introducing them to my kids.

Lord, I soaked my hearing aid and set my dentures on the counter by the sink. I hope this isn't a sign of what's to come. I need your help as soon as possible.

God, what became of my basket of laundry? I was sure I placed it on the floor next to the washing machine, but it's not there.

Lord, I just can't keep things straight. I circled January 7 on my calendar for the homeowners party, but when I showed up no one was there. Then I realized today is January 17! How did I miss 10 days?

Dear Father in heaven, please help me slow down. I jumped into my car this morning and didn't realize I was still in my pajamas until I pulled up in front of the grocery store.

Lord, my neighbor called to tell me I left my keys in the front door. It appears I'm practically inviting a thief to tea. Thank you for keeping me and my house safe.

God, can you believe it? Of course you can! I added a half-cup of milk instead of a whole cup to the pudding mix. No wonder it tasted like paste!

Dear Lord, I just dropped 10 holiday cards in the mailbox without proper postage and no return address labels. Please return my mind as soon as possible.

God, I was in a panic there for a minute because I thought my car had been stolen. Thank you for reminding me that I drove my daughter's truck to the hardware store.

Okay, Lord, I give up. I can't drink and drive—even soda pop. A sudden stop and I'm a wet and sticky mess.

I did it again, dear God. I answered the door after a persistent ringing of the doorbell, talked to the salesperson, and when I returned to the kitchen my grilled cheese sandwich had turned into a black brick.

Lord, thank you for your kindness
when I tried to back out of the garage
with the gear in Drive instead of Reverse.
I caught my mistake in the nick of time.

O Father in heaven, I wonder sometimes if you get fed up with my silly
ways—like yesterday when I drew a
blank when introducing my mother-in-
law to a new friend.

Can you imagine, Lord? I opened the
mail, shredded the stack of bills, and
filed the envelopes. What's going on?

This takes the cake, Father. I punched in my best friend's phone number, and when she answered I asked to speak to the manager.

How embarrassing, God. I asked for a refund at the cleaner's for a piece of lost clothing—only to find it a month later in the back of my closet. I returned the refund with a humble spirit.

Lord, I gave the bank teller my coffee gift card as proof of ID to get into my checking account. No wonder she looked at me with a wrinkled brow.

Where did I put my lunch? I was so sure I packed it in my shoulder bag. Oh, there it is, half assembled on the kitchen counter. Thank you for setting me straight, Lord.

Thank you, dear God, for helping me *before* I ordered a full diagnosis on my car. The culprit was a can of soda sloshing around under the driver's seat—not a strange problem with the engine.

Uh-oh! I nearly put on my husband's oversized shirt instead of my own. Lord, what would I do without your kind alerts? I'd be a mess.

Lord, I couldn't find my lip balm. I did a thorough house search until you guided my hand to my apron pocket. There it was—all these weeks. Thank you.

Father God, it does help to turn the iron to *on* when I want to press my clothes. "Cold press" works for olive oil but not for my best shirts. Thanks for pulling me out of my reverie.

I was so sure the TV was broken, Lord, until you reminded me to change the input back to "TV" after watching a DVD. It's a good thing you know how to operate everything.

Dear God, I wondered what was taking so long for the clothes to dry at the Laundromat. Yep, I hadn't inserted the proper coins. Thanks for rescuing me again.

Lord, what a surprise! The book I bought yesterday is identical to one I bought last month. I guess I'll make it a gift to a friend—but it's our secret, okay?

God, where is that ringing sound coming from? My desk drawer? What's my cell phone doing in there? Yep, another senior moment. God, please bless all my senior moments!

I reached for a box of tissue, Lord, and found a box of crackers instead. Oh my! Am I losing it that much?

Bank tellers don't accept payments for department store bills. Why didn't I realize what I was doing before looking so foolish? Maybe now I'll pay closer attention, Father God, with your help, that is.

Focus! Focus! I feel your reminders each day, dear God. Good thing since I almost tried to bake a cake in the freezer and freeze a batch of cookies in the oven.

Lord, thank you for overseeing my blunders—like my leaving the broiler on long after I finished cooking a steak. No fire thanks to you, but I did have a very hot kitchen!

God, I sent a condolence card instead of a birthday card to my neighbor. The front read "thinking of you," so I figured it was an all-purpose card—until she called to "thank" me for consoling her on her seventieth birthday. Thank you for giving her a sense of humor.

Father God, did I brush my teeth or brush my hair this morning? I'm not sure, so I'll start all over again—this time with you helping me keep my mind on what I'm doing. You know I need all the help I can get.

Oh, God, I did it this time. I bought a wedding gift instead of a baby shower gift. I hope the young mom will understand when she opens her present and finds a set of elegant candlesticks.

Lord, I just realized that I sprayed my neck and wrists with insect repellant instead of perfume. The bugs will stay away, sure, but people will too! Please give the people around me plenty of grace when they notice the outdoor odor.

God, I seem to be parking challenged… well, maybe parking lot challenged is more accurate. I pull my car into a space but can't find it when I return from the store. Will you be my personal navigation system from now on?

Dear Lord, I gave my daughter the same birthday gift two years in a row—and she didn't like it the first time! Will you remind me to check my gift-giving list next time?

Renting a car in England was a big mistake, God. I opened the front door on the left and panicked because I thought the steering wheel had been stolen. Oops! The Brits drive from the right-hand side!

It wasn't a good idea, Lord, for me to put in my contact lenses while working at the kitchen sink. I lost a lens down the disposal.

Where did all that water come from, God? Oh no! The garden hose has a tear and now the lawn is flooded. At least the grass won't be thirsty for a while.

Lord, people must have needed to hear your wisdom in your Word again because I just taught the same Sunday school lesson I did last week. How embarrassing, but at least I can trust you to make it worthwhile for everyone.

God, now what? I just emptied my purse of all the excess paper, gum wrappers, and old invoices, but now I can't find the $20 bill I had in there. Will you make sure whoever finds it uses it wisely?

Another oopsie, dear God. I just washed and dried my angora sweater with my cotton shirts. Now the sweater is sized to fit a doll. I need to slow down just like you've been telling me to do.

God, I love the pretty Christmas seals I received, but I put them on the envelopes where the postage stamps should be. And then I mailed them that way. When people have to pay the postage, please help them laugh good-naturedly at my mistake.

Thank you, Lord, for helping me snatch my toddler grandson out of the street and then giving me a hand when I fell at the curb.

Dear God, I praise your name! You always come through for me, and today was no exception. When I tried ice skating with the grandkids and crashed in the center of the rink, you kept me from breaking any bones. Hooray!

Lord, Fido doesn't respond when I call him in from the yard. Help me be patient with him—especially because I keep calling him Willie, the name of our previous dog.

Does saying no to pasta mean I can say yes to ice cream? I didn't think so. Thanks for clarifying my thinking, God.

Lord, thank you for reminding me to roll up the back window before I went through the self-serve car wash!

Okay, Father God, so I don't bake cookies anymore. I'm still good for something—eating the ones other people bake. Thank you for the ability to taste and enjoy sweet desserts!

Bouncing on the trampoline with my grandson wasn't a good idea. I see that now, heavenly Father, as I sit on the sidelines with a swollen ankle. Help me heal quickly.

The dogs are rebelling against the new food. Oh, no wonder! I've been giving them rabbit pellets. How did that happen? Lord, help me be more careful.

Yuck, Lord. White vinegar may look like water, but it sure doesn't smell like it. Good thing I filled only one glass before realizing my mistake.

Lord, I locked myself out of the house, and the spare key isn't where it should be. Oh, that's right, I gave it to my son, and he's on vacation. What should I do now?

A bowl of salt next to the coffee and cream? Whew! You alerted me in plenty of time. Sugar…sugar is what I meant to put out for my company.

It's a good excuse to go shopping, right Lord? We're 200 miles from home and I just now realized I forgot the hanging bag with our good clothes inside.

Like a cloud in the sky, that's me today, Lord. Not paying attention to what's going on, just floating along. I ate some fresh fruit salad…and then remembered I'm allergic to citrus fruits. Please keep my allergic reaction from being too severe.

Up the stairs or down? Which way am I going? Why am I going there? Lord, do I need to start writing myself notes for each moment of the day? I'd rather rely on you.

Father God, I tried to warm up my cup of coffee this morning—but I forgot to add the coffee. Hot cups are nice but not much use if they're empty.

A techie I'm not, dear God. I tried to locate a website by putting the address in an email box instead of the browser. Not good…

Thank you, Lord, for watching over me today when I put the TV remote in my purse instead of my cell phone.

Another senior moment, Father. Sigh.
I was going to drop off a bag of food at
the homeless shelter, but when I arrived
I realized the bag was filled with empty
containers for the recycling center. That
means I put the bag of food at the curb
for recycling! I need your help every day.

Lord, we tested our patience and the
new smoke alarm today by broiling meat
too long. Thanks for reminding us to
open the windows to let in the fresh, cool
air.

Last call for boarding? I was sitting at the flight gate for an hour and never heard the announcement. Oh! The departure time and gate changed and I didn't notice. Please give me your grace and the airline people patience. It seems I can't do a thing without your guidance— but that's good, isn't it?

Lord, today I freaked out about my vision—that is, until you reminded me that maybe my glasses just needed cleaning. Thank you for that.

Today I blew it, Father God. I handed a panhandler on a street corner a $50 bill and asked for change. He stuffed the money in his pocket, shrugged, and sat down. I drove off, my face flushed with embarrassment.

Lord, I wondered why my potted plants died while I was on vacation. Then I realized I'd locked the gate to the backyard so my neighbor couldn't get to them. Thank you for bringing that to mind *before* I complained.

Of all the nerve, God. The clerk at the grocery store refused my credit card. But when I looked at it I realized I'd handed her my AARP membership card. Not too swift!

Whipped cream on a baked potato? Something new around here. And probably not the last weird thing I'll eat given my record lately. Well, at least I noticed my error before putting sour cream on the baked apples. Thanks for checking up on me, Lord. I love that about you.

God, turning east when I meant to turn west took me 10 miles out of the way today. But when it comes to directions, I thank you for putting my sins as far from you as east is from west like it says in Psalm 103. That's a good thing!

God, I wondered why the house was so cold this morning. I forgot to close the window before going to bed even though it was on my to-do list. I guess I need to check that list every day. Thank you for keeping me safe all night.

Uh-oh! We cut the grass before pulling the weeds. God, can you believe the ridiculous things we do sometimes? Help us, please, with these pesky senior moments.

I just dumped six of my own books into the library return slot before I realized it. Lord, I'm praying there's a way to get them back. I'll stop by the desk as soon as the library opens tomorrow.

The store clerk refused my payment today—and then I realized I'd handed her pesos. Of course they don't work in the U.S.

Lord, I can't steam veggies if I forget to put water in the pot. What was I thinking…er, not thinking, actually.

Father in heaven, thank you for having the neighbor check on us. We left the garage door open two nights this week, feeling sure we'd locked up tight. Thank you for having her call us.

Lord, did I just save myself a bundle or not? I paid my MasterCard balance twice. I can outwit myself sometimes if I'm not careful.

O God, I need help with my calendar. I put out the flag for Columbus Day but it's Valentine's Day.

Lord, I'm not much for telling jokes, but I was really pathetic this morning when I started a joke but couldn't finish because I forgot the ending. Help me be silent unless I have something to say that is worth listening to.

Our roof has a leak, dear God, and I'm suddenly aware after dialing the phone that calling an appliance repairman isn't the right solution.

Lord, thank you for reminding me that laughter—not aspirin—is the best medicine. I'm going to put the pill away and smile instead.

Dear God, I had a memory lapse today, but I'm not giving up on myself. I know I can rely on you to supply the right words when I need them, especially when they're "I love you" and "Please forgive me."

Lord, I called my brother by the wrong name this morning. Thank you for teaching him about forgiveness.

O God, last week I wrapped Christmas gifts for my grandson and granddaughter. When the kids opened them on Christmas Eve, my granddaughter wondered why I'd given her a video game geared for boys, and my grandson was surprised to open a boxed necklace and earring set! I guess I mixed up the name tags. Thank you for grandkids who love me, mistakes and all.

Lord, if it weren't for the sand at the bottom of the slide I'd have broken my hip. I need to take it easier when I play with my grandkids. I'm not as young as I used to be, for sure.

God, I was sure I told my sister to meet me on Cedar Street for coffee and dessert at Sandy's. How could she mistake the invitation as cider and sandwiches at Cedar's? She's old, that's how. Or was it my mistake? I'm not so young anymore either. I'll never know because we didn't meet.

Father in heaven, I was more than surprised to find sunflowers springing up where I was sure I hadn't planted anything because I wanted to put in a rock garden. Still, the sunflowers are pretty so I'll enjoy them.

God, I thought this was where the "Enter Freeway" ramp was, but the sign says "Exit." Thank you for keeping me from a potentially horrifying mistake. Please show me where the on-ramp is.

Lord, my checking account is empty. How can this be? Oh! I subtracted instead of added in the ledger. Whew!

Where, oh where are my glasses, dear God? Where oh where could they be? I need them fast. Oh, look on top of my head, you say? You're always right. Thank you.

I know how to handle these memory lapses, Lord. Start leaving myself reminder notes. Now if I'll just remember to read them.

Today I'm going to do things in the right order: say my prayers, get out of bed, get dressed, eat breakfast…ummm…say my prayers, get out of bed, get dressed, eat breakfast…say my prayers, get out of bed, get dressed, eat breakfast…I give up, Lord. What comes next?

Thank you, Lord, for a lovely evening of moonlight and starlight and the chance to ponder your beautiful creation after a busy day of doing…well, hmmm…of doing not one thing I can remember at this moment.

Dear God, sometimes I want to kick up my heels and dance, but these bones just want to sit down in a comfy chair and watch *Dancing with the Stars.* Help me do both—at separate times, of course.

Lord, I have an answer for these senior moments—laugh and take them with a grain of sugar.

Dear God, today I took a bad spill and fell into worry and fear. You scooped me up into your loving arms, and I'm okay now. Thank you!

Father, when I walk with you I don't trip or lose my balance. You are my solid rock—the One on whom I can always rely. Thank you for putting Psalm 18:2 in the Bible so I know that for sure.

Today, O Lord, I'm leaving behind my old baggage—guilt and grief—and picking up gratitude.

Thank you, God, that in your eyes I'm a pearl of great price, regardless of how my luster might look to others. Thank you for including that in your Word—in Matthew 13:45-46.

Father, thank you for the good reminder to release myself from other people's opinions and to trust in you alone, especially when I goof up.

God, how I thank you for helping me remember to add instead of subtract when I was doing my taxes today. A mistake would be a disaster.

How funny that I spent three hours smiling behind a costume party mask only to realize at home that no one could see *my* face—only the face on the mask. Talk about a senior moment and a sore mouth! Thanks for laughing with me, dear God.

God, this is getting bad. Today I couldn't find the sweater my spouse knitted for me for my birthday. I panicked until I undressed for bed and discovered I'd been wearing it all day!

Lord, how do I get my hands and arms and sense of balance to work together when I want to carry a tray of food from the kitchen to the dining room? I need you to steady me.

Dear God, I'm about to give up on notepaper and buy a smart phone so I can keep track of my tasks on an app. Or will the same thing happen? I'll set down the phone and forget where I put it? Sometimes I feel hopeless! I'm glad you never give up on me.

Father in heaven, thanks for reminding me that Proverbs 17:22 says, "A cheerful heart is good medicine." I needed to hear that again, especially today when I'm down in the dumps over dropping my new camera into the water while shooting pictures of my grandkids surfing.

I lost the left sock of my favorite pair today, Lord. I paid $18 for *real* cashmere to keep my feet warm. What do I do with only one sock? Oops! Here is the missing one—tangled in a shirt in the dryer.

I wanted to hurry my summer tan along, Lord, with a bit of self-tanning lotion. I just discovered the bottle of liquid I chose won't do the trick. It's after-bath moisturizing lotion. Help me find my glasses, please.

You're a good speaker," a woman remarked as she paused before leaving the meeting room. Okay, I'll accept the compliment, dear God. But did she have to add that I look a lot older than when she saw me last year?

Why can't I remember whether I brushed my teeth? I need an angel to remind me, Lord. I went back and forth to the bathroom half a dozen times at least, debating the entire time whether I did or didn't. Finally, I brushed—perhaps again—just to be sure.

If I want to keep track of my papers, I shouldn't set them on the kitchen counter while cooking on my gas stove. You got it, Lord! I had a close call when the top one caught fire. Thank you for reminding me to keep a towel handy. I used it to snuff out the flames.

The living room felt extra warm today. I took off my sweater and started fanning my face, Lord, when suddenly I remembered I'd forgotten to turn off the broiler after cooking burgers two hours ago.

No wonder my friend wrinkled her nose when she lifted her teacup to her lips. I made the pot of tea using my glass coffee-pot. Not a good idea, dear God. We had a good laugh over the coffee-flavored tea, and I made a fresh pot. I had a red face, I'm sure.

So much for soufflé. I found out today, Lord, it's best to eat it when it's hot and fresh—not the next day after letting it sit in the oven for 24 hours. At least the oven was on a timer, so the soufflé didn't burn to a crisp. I need to walk around with an alarm clock.

I got into a peck of trouble today, Father. When I was asked for my driver's license to verify my account at the bank, the teller pointed out that it was expired! I've been driving around for two weeks without a license. Thank you for this alert and for keeping me safe. Please give me extra grace as I deal with the people at the Department of Motor Vehicles first thing tomorrow.

What's this, O God? The missing slice of cake from last night's dinner party! I wondered where my slice went. Apparently it slipped between the stove and counter when I was serving our guests. At least that mystery is solved—though I never did get a taste of the cake.

Lord, I was so proud of myself for catching the lone hair on my chin and plucking it out before anyone noticed it. If only I'd seen the one above my lip at the same time. Unfortunately, my friend did and told me about it as graciously as she could. Thanks for listening to my embarrassing moment.

Eek! Lord, I could barely whisper let alone talk when I discovered a mouse under the kitchen sink and another one racing across the floor. I took a deep breath and then screamed for my husband. Is this a senior thing or a female thing?

I seem to be directionally challenged these days, O God. My navigation system tells me I'm going north but it *feels* like I'm going south or east. Today I went with my feelings, and they took me an hour out of my way. Thank you for helping me relax and explore a new area.

Leftover lasagna tastes great warmed in the oven—but I'll never know now because after leaving the restaurant I put the carryout box on top of my car while inserting my key in the door lock…and then got in and drove off. By the time I remembered it and stopped, it was long gone. Lord, I need your watchful eye on me during these senior years.

Dear God, who is to blame when my spouse and I both have hearing challenges? I heard myself say we'd meet for lunch at Friday's, but my wife said she heard me say Freddy's. We finally connected by cell phone and decided to eat at home.

Mistakes are hard to admit, Lord, but admit them I must. The other day when my husband asked me to mail a bill payment and deliver a note to our neighbor, I got distracted. Sure enough, I handed the bill to John next door and dropped the note meant for him into a mailbox.

Lord, as you know six ladies showed up at my door tonight for a movie and dessert. I could hardly contain my surprise and delight! Then I looked at the kitchen calendar and realized I'd organized the evening and offered to host it! Quick as a bunny I put on the coffeepot and pulled out some cookies and ice cream.

Lord, this is the last time I grocery shop with two preschool grandchildren. I loaded my cart as fast as I could but then I had to leave it behind as I ran after the boys so they wouldn't dart into the parking lot. Will you keep my cart safe until I get back to it?

Is it Bob or Bill or Brett? I'm not good with names. Today I seemed to be at my worst, God. I was attempting to introduce my brother-in-law—a man I've known for 30 years!—and I couldn't get his name right.

Dear heavenly Father, one way to keep veggies crisp is to cook them on a broken burner like I did last night. Once more I neglected to check to make sure everything was working. I did think it was odd that the pot wasn't steaming though.

Someone once said the best place to look for a lost item is where you least expect it. That happened to my husband on Saturday. His missing carpentry nails were hanging out of his mouth—just where he'd put them! He tried to put the blame on me…and I was reminded how often I do that to you, dear God.

Lord, it seems simple enough. If I want to keep my small office cozy and warm, it would help to turn the space heater *on* and make sure the cord is plugged in. What a concept. I'll have to give it a try so I can take off my jacket and gloves.

Lord, can you imagine? I listened as George, a friend from the tennis club, relayed the news that his wife had suffered a stroke and gone to heaven. Pete, who has a hearing problem piped up, "Havana? Nice place to go. I hope she has a good time." Thank you for gracious and understanding friends.

A coffee gift card will buy a cup of coffee, but it won't buy a blouse at JC Penney's even though I tried. Oh, Lord, I need a refresher course in how to focus!

God, it seemed like a good idea at the time—taking my granddaughter to a movie and out to dinner. But when she looked at me with a puzzled expression and I felt my face flush with embarrassment, I knew I'd made a mistake. I should have only considered G-rated movies instead of G and PG-13.

I tucked a gift card into my grandson's birthday card but when he saw it, his face turned sour. O Lord, it was for a baby's clothing store when it should have been for a game store. I wonder what my niece, a new mom, will think when she opens her envelope and finds a gift card for a game store.

Dear God, some of my favorite moments as a senior are cuddling on the couch with my husband and munching on popcorn while watching a good mystery—even if I don't always keep track of the plot. Thank you for making my life so comfortable.

What fun I had today going down the slide at the park with my grandson. I made it all the way to the bottom and ended up with a bit of sand in my jeans but a lot of laughter in my heart. I praise you for giving us the gifts of love and joy.

I enjoyed being asked if I'm a senior at the store today. I said yes with confidence and took joy in receiving a 10 percent discount on my purchases. Lord, thank you for showing me another positive aspect of being older.

God, do birds and squirrels and mice have senior moments if they live a long time? I'm giggling at the thought. I think I'll hang out in my yard today and see what they're up to.

One thing about these senior moments and days, Lord: I can travel as often as I like—even if it's just around the block. My imagination takes me to faraway places, and I'm back home again in less than an hour.

This morning at seven o'clock, I showed up for the Sunrise Special at a local café only to find out that I was 10 hours early. The *Sunset* Special isn't available until five o'clock. Lord, I need new glasses!

Today I'm happy to be a senior, Lord. Many people don't live long enough to find out what it's like to hang out in their pajamas all day if they want to.

I lost at bingo today, Lord, but I won a new friend at the senior center. I count the day a blessing even though I hate to lose a competition.

God, for my age, how do I look in your eyes? I know I can count on you to tell me the truth. You say you love your people even to their old age no matter their limitations. Thank you for that. I feel much better now.

Lord, I'm so grateful for the precious moments I have with friends over lunch or tea. As we share the good times and the not-so-good times, we rest in the knowledge that you are in charge. You're an amazing, loving God.

My dog and I are just a couple of oldies enjoying the day together as we walk and talk in our own special ways. Thank you for creating so many wonderful creatures.

Today, Lord, I had another senior moment. However, my memory's not too good these days, so I've already forgotten what it was!

I tried skateboarding this weekend and nearly landed on my bottom at the end of a hilly street. Thank you, God, for rescuing me from a fast exit off the planet.

No boyfriends for me right now, so on Valentine's Day I'm going to buy myself a bouquet of flowers and a box of candy. That's one of the privileges of being comfortable where I'm at.

Being a senior has its perks! We can take out our hearing aids when we talk to ourselves. I did that today, Lord. I'd rather listen to you, and I don't need technology for that.

Thank you, Lord, for giving me second thoughts when I was about to add sugar to my meat and salt on the dessert. It's all about focus, isn't it?

God, I was a bit chagrined today when I put on the kettle for tea and then went for a walk. Thank you for leading me back home the moment I remembered and for keeping my house safe.

Lord, thanks for reminding me that it's always okay to say "I love you"—even if I've said it several times already today but don't remember.

Dear God, today people must have thought I was one card short of a full deck. I backed out of a parking space and narrowly missed hitting a light post. Thank you for saving me from an embarrassing moment, and a huge bill, and maybe a lawsuit, and…and…

Lord, sour cream on oatmeal doesn't taste as good as vanilla yogurt on oatmeal. I shouldn't have used a yogurt carton for storing the leftover sour cream.

Father God, how funny life can be!
When I invited my neighbor to go window shopping with me, she wondered
which windows I'd broken!

My friend and I spent the afternoon
watching an old movie. It was fun to see
the film again, although right now I can't
recall the title, the plot, or the names of
the hero and heroine. But we had a good
time, Lord. Thank you for blessing me
with such a good friend.

Dear God, a man at our seniors club said he won a small part in a community play. "I'm not much more than a doorknob in the third act," he quipped. His wife shot back, "An easy part—no acting required!" That conversation reminded me that sometimes I'm a "doorknob" when it comes to stepping out for you, Lord. I'd rather hang back, pretending I'm not a vital resource for you, instead of declaring my faith in you with courage and joy. Please help me make a difference for you.

Dear God, sometimes I get annoyed with myself. I'm sure glad you're so patient and understanding. Just this morning when I poured shredded wheat into a pot of hot water I wondered why the oatmeal I'd planned to eat wasn't turning out right.

I'm so glad I can turn to you, Lord, when I goof up. You set me straight as you did yesterday when I loaned my English-speaking neighbor a book written in French.

It's fun to share humorous experiences, but not such fun when I forget the point and leave the audience hanging like I did at the women's club meeting last week. Father, I'm so glad you give me the courage to go on when I mess up like that.

Lord, how could I send a congratulations card to my friend when I meant to choose a sympathy card because her husband died? I knew they were having trouble in their marriage, but I didn't mean to take my support to that extreme. Please help her see the humor in the situation.

God, I think you're telling me to forgive myself when I pull a blunder. Do you really mean it? Even when I forget to put oil in the popcorn popper?

Dear Lord, on my way to the bathroom at two o'clock this morning I tripped over the walker I'd left in the hallway. Thank you for getting me back into bed without a broken bone.

God, I see my reflection in the mirror and it's pretty shocking. I'm glad I'm still around, but next time I'll take off my glasses before I look at myself.

Three cheers, Lord, for the top 10 beneficial items in my life: a cane, pain pills, sturdy shoes, banisters, an elevated toilet seat, bathtub safety handles, a nonskid bathmat, a staircase chairlift, a walker, and your amazing Word.

Help me today, Father. I said yes to seeing a movie with a friend at the senior center, but we never connected. She called me from the Center for Seniors at our community college wondering where I was. Oh dear!

So I followed his advice and ate peppermint ice cream and key lime pie. I'm sorry today though because I don't feel so great. Lord, thank you for letting me come to you even when my predicament is my fault.

I'm so grateful for the comfort found in Proverbs 3:24: "When you lie down, you will not be afraid; when you lie down, your sleep will be sweet." Thank you, God, for reassuring me when I'm afraid of not waking up.

Lord, today I'm feeding my mind with crossword puzzles and feeding my body with…well, okay, I'll put away the chocolate and eat an apple.

Imagine that, dear God! My young neighbor said she wants to be like me when she grows up. Really? I wonder if she took a good look? Wrinkles, spider veins, thinning hair, and hearing aids don't seem that appealing. Is she seeing you in me, Lord?

Lord, I'm grateful that you love me just as I am this minute—sitting in my pajamas and watching a movie when I should be cleaning my house.

I said no today—the first time in a long time. I don't want to sit on a committee, attend a meeting, or collect money door-to-door for a good cause. At least not today. Right now I want to say yes to you and simply *be* for at least 24 hours.

I'm thankful for my senior years, for this season of life you've given me, Lord. I'm even thankful for the occasional senior moments once I get over the embarrassment. I'm all grown up, and I can let go of what others think of me—even when I answer the door in my bathrobe.

I splurged, dear Father, and bought a pair of silver sandals for going to the Friday night dance with Henry. When we arrived, I wanted to hit him over the head with one of the shoes. It was an evening of line dancing—and everyone was wearing jeans and western boots! I guess men have their senior moments too!

Okay, Lord, today was the last straw. I turned to my husband and said, "Charles, tell the joke about…" and then gave away the punch line. Poor Charles didn't know what to do…until everyone realized what happened and had a good laugh.

Lord, I felt like cashing in the day with a click of the DELETE key on my computer keyboard. I lost my credit card, received a parking ticket, and forgot my daughter's birthday. I'm going to call it a night. Dear Father in heaven, give me a peaceful rest. I'll see you in the morning.

Dear God, I'm chuckling at something I read this morning. A couple in their eighties decided to get married. They asked the local drugstore manager if they could use his store for their bridal registry.

Lord, I don't have the energy to grow any older. Someone once said it takes everything you've got to get old. Well, everything I had got up and went, so please help me make it through another day.

My husband complained one time too many about my cooking. You'll be so proud of me, Lord. I didn't argue this time. I just agreed with him, resigned my chief cook position, and told him he could take over kitchen duty effective immediately. As far as I can tell, we're having takeout for dinner tonight.

Lord, how could the policeman give me a ticket for parking in a "parking pass only" zone? I put my pass in the driver's window as requested. Was it my fault that I accidentally used a movie pass instead? It was an honest mistake!

Lord, I need help remembering the names of my husband's business friends, so I've created reminders to help me: Funny-face Fred, Baldheaded Bob, and so on. But my idea backfired at the latest office party when I walked up to Fred and realized I couldn't pull his name out of my brain for the life of me. Suddenly I got it! "Hello, Funny-face Fred," I blurted. I wanted to crawl out of the room. Hopefully my husband still has a job.

Lord, I had quite a moment today when my granddaughter touched my face and said she was glad I was old. I asked her why, and she said it's because my cheeks are so soft. Now I'm glad I'm old too.

Lord, my husband misplaced his keys again. He got mad when he couldn't find them, and he blamed me. I don't see it as my fault just because they were in my purse. I think he's just getting old and can't remember that he put them there. At least I'm pretty sure he did.

Dear God, I had a different kind of senior moment. Instead of forgetting or misplacing something I just sat in my yard and focused on the sunrise without thinking of all the things I had on my to-do list. This is one of the blessings of having time to relax and appreciate what happens around me.

Thank you, dear Lord. Each day I pray for wisdom and understanding, and you answer me in abundance so I'm not afraid to keep going.

Father in heaven, a new friend I met on a bus shared her terrific senior moment. May I have one just like it someday. She was going home from her college reunion where she was honored for being the oldest living alumnus at age 101!

This week I welcomed my first great-grandbaby! Thank you, Lord, for this ultimate senior moment.

Lord, my husband is going a bit far with these senior moments. Every day he has at least 20 of them, I'm sure. It's called napping.

Dear God, what a moment! I prayed for grace in an awkward situation, and you poured it out. I feel renewed. Thank you for helping me make it this far in life.

God, thank you so much for calling me to mentor a younger woman. My times with her are among the highlights of my senior years so far.

How special it was, dear God, to have my grandson help me up when I lost my balance and fell off my bicycle. Maybe I should retire my bike and buy a three-wheeler…

Here's a moment to remember, Lord. I asked my neighbor if I could borrow a wrap for tonight. She came over an hour later with a frozen chicken-and-cheese wrap. I had something different in mind—a shawl to wear over my dance dress.

Lord, I'm realizing that the best way to handle my senior moments is to admit them instead of dodging them. Thank you for helping me do so with a sense of humor.

Today, dear God, you can call me Snow White. I woke up this morning and was shocked to find my hair is whiter than ever. What a moment. I had fooled myself into thinking I had more time before looking that old.

Lord, what do I do when my own husband forgets my name? To me that's the colossal senior moment. I never expected this to happen when I married ole… *ummm*…ole whatshisname!

Thank you, Father God, for being here with me when I get confused and scared, when I become a victim of my age instead of a victor because of what Jesus has done for me.

Lord, I asked my friend to keep a secret. She agreed, reminding me that even a moment after I share my secret she often forgets what I've said. She's a senior after all!

Dear God, today a yellow jacket nearly stung my husband as he snoozed in the yard. I warned him to pay attention so he could avoid being stung. He sat up and shouted, "Out of here, you yellow coat!" We both broke out laughing.

Lord, here's one senior moment I don't really mind. My husband and I can watch a movie together, and whether we've seen it before or not doesn't matter because we can't remember the plot.

God, thank you for keeping us close to you even to our old age and white hair—and that includes all our senior moments!

O God, I need an inputting lesson. I sent my friend a birthday email today congratulating her on reaching her sixtieth year. Unfortunately, I missed the date by 10 years. She just turned 50! Please do what you can to reinstate our friendship.

Lord, how grateful I am for a cozy night with grandkids all around me. We're sipping sodas and eating popcorn. This is definitely a senior moment worth celebrating.

Today, my God, I made a real blunder. I buttered my bread without paying attention. Imagine my tongue's surprise when it didn't taste margarine…but a mouthful of bacon grease I'd stored in an empty margarine tub.

This morning it was freezing, Lord, so I grabbed a scarf off a hook in the closet and threw it around my neck. Just before walking out the door, I saw my reflection in the mirror and realized I'd picked one of my husband's ties.

Dear God, please help me with the luncheon I'm serving tomorrow. I get so nervous when I entertain. Remember the afternoon I served tuna salad on fresh lettuce and then discovered after everyone had gone that by mistake I'd used the cheap tuna I feed to the cat?

Lord, so much for romantic dancing in the dark. I stubbed my toe and stepped on my husband's new shoes. Lights on from now on or no dancing.

Father in heaven, I took my neighbor a basket of fresh oranges this morning, and when I got home I realized they were the same ones she'd brought me a few days ago!

How embarrassing, God. I jumped into a white truck in the store parking lot while waiting for my husband to finish some shopping. I panicked when a stranger slid into the driver's seat and asked if I needed anything. That's when I realized I was in *his* truck not ours. Needless to say, I made a quick exit.

Oh my! Lord, today I reached for a glue stick instead of lipstick. Thanks to you I caught my mistake before I glued my lips together.

Talk about doing too much in one day! Lord, I walked up to the teller in the bank, pointed to my grocery list, and asked if she knew where the crackers were. She smiled and said, "We don't have any groceries here, but you can take out some cash to take to the supermarket."

My elderly neighbor was about to celebrate her ninetieth birthday. She chuckled when she opened the card I gave her at her party, congratulating her on graduating from high school. Oops! My niece is going to be shocked to get a happy ninetieth birthday wish! She can hold onto it for the next few decades.

Dear God, I'm remembering a tender moment in my mother's life when she told me, "All I can give you are roots and wings." I hope I did that for my children too. Thank you for overseeing our parenting from birth through adulthood.

Lord, thank you for watching over all my comings and goings, especially when I plan to go north and discover I'm heading south.

Today I baked a cake and when it collapsed in the middle I remembered what Aunt Mary did in a similar moment. She cut the cake into cubes and served it with fruit and whipped cream on top. Thank you for bringing that to mind, Lord. That's what I did, and it was a huge hit.

I'm grateful that most of my tears shed during these older years are from a heart filled with joy. Thank you, God, for giving me a moment-by-moment appreciation of the life you've given me.

Lord, I forgot my cane at my friend's house so when I went out today I grabbed an old mop handle instead. Some may call this a senior moment. I call it being creative.

I put my name-tag sticker on my jacket and proceeded into the meeting room. Someone pointed out that it was upside down. I did some quick thinking, thanks to you, Lord, and quipped, "I did that on purpose so I won't forget who I am."

Lord, I decided to stand tall today. When my six-foot, three-inch son-in-law arrived, I stood on a chair to give him a hug.

Heavenly Father, I found two concert tickets in my jacket pocket today. I whooped for joy until I read the date—last year! I'd wondered where they went! Thanks for solving that mystery though I'm sorry I missed the event.

Dear God, some senior moments aren't all that funny to those of us who have them. They're an indicator that we're growing old. I guess that's a good thing since few people live long enough to enjoy the privilege.

Thank you, Lord, for the best senior
moment of all—really getting that *you*
are in charge and I'm not.

How embarrassing, Father. Today when
I ran into my tennis partner in the supermarket I thanked her for her "apathy"
instead of her "empathy" on the news
of my mother's death. No wonder she
looked at me so strangely.

Lord, today my husband announced
that he'd just purchased two rowboats—
one for him and one for me—to use on
the lake this summer. I asked why two.
He reminded me that when he gets bossy
I always tell him to row his own boat.

Dear God, there is one good thing about listening to books on CD or through media at my age. The stories go in one ear, I enjoy them, and then they go out the other ear so I can read them again later with the same enjoyment.

Lord, someone told me that peanut butter on banana slices is delicious. I don't like peanut butter, so I tried just plain butter. Not so good. But thank you for giving me the willingness to try something different.

Dear God, thank you for letting me know in your Word, in John 10:10 specifically, that you give me life in all its fullness—right on through the senior moments and up to my last breath.

Father in heaven, today I felt shaky so I reached out to you, and you offered me a nearby tree for support. Thank you.

I made a hole-in-one today, dear God, by tossing an orange peel from the kitchen table to the garbage disposal. Not bad for an old gal, right?

God, what an experience for my friend Mimi today. Her granddaughter told her a joke, and she laughed so hard her front dentures came loose and fell into her hand. Bless her and comfort her, dear Lord. A roomful of people saw this embarrassing incident.

I nearly made a trip to the emergency room today, Lord. I fell off a swing at the park. My grandchildren and I were having a contest to see who could reach the highest point. Yes, I lost…

Lord, today the clerk at the store gave me a funny look when I asked for a dozen hens instead of a dozen eggs.

How strange is it, God, that I made our bed in the middle of the night? I woke up and my husband was gone, so I assumed I'd overslept and he'd gone to work. That is, until he returned from the bathroom and wondered what in thunder I was up to.

Lord, once more I parked in my neighbor's garage (with his permission) to make room for my husband's work truck in ours. The next morning when I woke up, I called the police because I thought someone had stolen my car. What a public blunder! Help me cope with the embarrassment.

This afternoon, heavenly Father, I couldn't figure out how to open the door to my motel room. The clerk at the front desk reminded me that I needed a key *card*, not a regular key. Oh for the good old days when a key in a lock opened a door.

The cats are up to no good, Lord. They keep scratching and meowing to be let in, but we don't own any cats!

I like the new sweater Edna gave me for my birthday but, Lord, I'm sure it's the same color as the one I bought for her. Oh! Is this a case of re-gifting? Now what should I do?

I'm sure I took a class in this room before, God. It looks so familiar. Oh, I remember! I've already taken this class—in this room and with the same instructor! I'd better get out of here and ask for a refund. These senior moments are starting to really sneak up on me.

Lord, how frustrating to bring along a disposable camera for a special occasion and then discover it won't take pictures because this is the second time I've tried to use it? Thanks for waking me up to what's going on so I won't get really upset.

Dear God, what does it mean to "sleep like a dog"? My dog wakes me up at least twice each night. To me that's a dog's life, which isn't one I want to copy.

This is the last time I buy two pairs of the same style shoe but in different colors. I've yet to put on a matching pair! Back to the optometrist first thing Monday morning.

I can't believe it, Father. How could I mistake a kitchen sponge for a slice of bread and pop it into the toaster? Boy did it stink when it started to burn!

Today my muscles rebelled when I got out of bed and tried to stand. I promised them a massage at the end of the day if they cooperated. They're still thinking about it! Father in heaven, please help me get through this day.

What is that sticky note on the fridge door? Oh yes—a reminder to buy bread and eggs at the store. Why didn't I check the fridge before I went to the store? Looks like I need your assistance on every front, God.

Not good, dear God! I found a library book in the den. It was due back six months ago. Now I owe a big fine, and I haven't even read it yet…or have I and I just don't remember?

Lord, I almost passed along some neighborhood gossip today. Then I suddenly realized I was about to tell the very person about whom the gossip was being passed. Thank you for reminding me what Ephesians 4:29 says: "Do not let any unwholesome talk come out of your mouths."

My friend and I got stuck in the middle of the lake today, dear God. Thank you for sending the Coast Guard to rescue us. Next time no sailing without enough fuel for the motor in case the wind dies down, which is what happened this time. We were about to ask you to help us walk on water so we could reach shore when you sent help.

Yep, Lord, today was dumb thing number 316. I put birdseed in the rabbit hutch and rabbit pellets into the bird feeder. So far neither animal has complained.

I locked myself out of my neighbor's house by leaving the key on her kitchen counter. I'm supposed to water her plants for a month while she's on vacation. Lord, will you help me get hold of her and help us find a solution to this problem?

July 10 is the date I set for lunch at my house with my book club, Lord. Why then, did everyone turn up on June 10 when I wasn't even home? Imagine, all those women having the same senior moment at the same time!

Lord, I like butter on my popcorn but not in my pocket. How did a stick of butter land there? I have a feeling I'll never find out unless you tell me.

Dear God, there are senior moments and then there are senior moments. They're not funny when they jeopardize our safety—as was the case last night when my husband forgot to put out the fire in the fireplace even though he promised me he had. I guess we'll have to double-check each other from now on.

Lord, I looked all over the house and garage for the photo my sister said she'd sent me of our mother when she was in college. Turns out it wasn't one of Mom but of Ron, our brother. Off to the audiologist for a hearing test!

God, what do people mean when they say something is "good for a laugh"? Are they laughing with me or at me? I can't always tell.

Lord, I just found an invitation to a wedding that occurred last year. Is it too late to send a response and a gift? Do you think the friendship is over?

Today, God, I tried to dry some rugs at a neighborhood Laundromat. It would have been fine if I'd put them in a dryer that worked. Next time I'll try to remember to check to make sure the dryer is turning before I sit down and read my book.

Lord, I tested some new makeup today, but I should have stuck with my usual, reliable brand and color. I emerged looking like I was wearing war paint.

I am grateful today, dear Father, for the wisdom you give me, especially during these senior moments. I wouldn't make it through some of them without you.

Lord, my husband nearly choked when I told him I'd spent $1000 while shopping today. "*Window* shopping, that is," I added with a grin. Then he calmed down, and we both had a good laugh.

Today, I looked in the mirror and thought, *I have crow's feet around my eyes, and my neck is as loose as a goose's. I'm not bad looking for an old bird.* Thank you for keeping me under your wing, my dear God.

Ah, sweet memories, Lord, of times and places from the past when life was simple and carefree. Today I will make new memories, one moment at a time, so I can look back on them tomorrow or next week or next year and be grateful and glad for them as well.

Lord, I love knowing that each day—despite my senior moments—will be the best yet because you are with me.

Lord, what a blessing that through you
I can forgive myself for my mistakes and
faux pas and focus instead on grace-filled
moments.

Today, Father God, I ate pistachios and
chocolate for lunch, along with a cup of
green tea. A silly meal, yes, but a lot of
fun. Thank you for smiling with me.

How embarrassing that I called my
friend Allen by the name of the street
he lives on—Rose. Lord, I'm so glad you
always know my name.

Hearing correctly is a challenge these days, God. Someone asked today at lunch if I like fish and I said, "No, I prefer tennis." She's probably still wondering what I thought she'd said.

Lord, should I be thankful or hurt when younger women say I look good for my age? I want to run to the mirror and check for myself.

How blessed I am, dear God, that my granddog loves me no matter what— even when I attach his leash to his collar incorrectly and he gets tangled up.

I could use some help, Lord, especially when I try to turn on the TV with my cell phone. When am I going to learn how to use all these electronic gizmos without messing up?

Another oops today. I typed a website address into the "to" box of an email client and wondered why the message wouldn't send!

What a blessing, dear God, to be able to focus on the moment I'm living instead of the ones coming down the pike. I know I can trust you for my future.

Today, I need to hold on to you, God, because I've faced one senior moment after another this morning. From leaving the stove on after cooking to losing the garage door opener, from misplacing my hearing aid to forgetting my hair appointment, it's been a rough time. Maybe I should return to bed and start all over, pretending this day never happened.

I'm going to settle in tonight and watch an old film. That will keep me out of trouble, Lord, as long as I can figure out how to stream from Netflix to my computer. Oh, for the good old days when I could just drive to the cinema, buy a ticket, sit down, and enjoy a good movie.

Someone said baked Alaska is delicious.
What a strange thing to say about a state.
Am I missing something, Lord?

Lord, where in the world did I get the
idea I could jump rope at my age? A big
bruise on my backside is telling me I
shouldn't have tried. Live and learn—
I am and I did.

Lord, I don't feel so bad about senior
moments these days. Even my grandkids
are doing some odd things. Today they're
tweeting instead of talking. The last I
heard, tweeting was for birds!

I'm relieved that in these uncertain times in my life Psalm 119 reminds me that your Word is "a lamp for my feet, a light on my path." Thank you for being with me no matter what.

Lord, why did my friend look at me funny when I told her I played miniature golf with my grandson and scored a putt? Okay, so I don't get all the lingo. At least I'm staying active and involved.

I saw an ad for a "mature" driver's course for people over 50. I've been driving for 60 years. I think I'm plenty mature by now, don't you think so too, Lord?

I can make my own decisions, but first I have to find out what I need to decide. Help me, Lord. I'm feeling like another senior moment is upon me.

My niece told me the other day that I'm amazing for a woman my age. I was quick to tell her that if that's true, it's only because of your amazing grace, God.

Getting older and being retired gives me time to do more of the things I enjoy, such as hiking and knitting. Thank you, Lord, for giving me time for recreation. Now, Lord, if you will help me experience fewer senior moments, such as forgetting where I put my car keys or where I laid my eyedrops, I'd sure appreciate it.

Lord, I put my grandbaby down for a nap but it seems I'm the one who needed to sleep. I dozed off in the chair next to her crib. When I woke up I was relieved to see her smiling at me through the slats. Seniors and babies have a lot in common.

Dear God, I have an idea for a new career—but at the moment I can't remember what it is. I'll get back to you on that.

I know this sounds hard to believe, but I have never been on eBay—not even out of curiosity. Does that make me an oddity? So what else is new? I've been surprising myself and others with moments more surprising than this one. Lord, help me point someone toward you every day.

Dear God, one of the things I like best about the senior years is they bring me closer to spending eternity with you.

I skipped to the corner in the rain with my granddaughter. With her hand in mine, I didn't worry about falling. I felt like a child again, and it was a wonderful moment for both of us. Thank you, Lord.

One nice thing about this time of life, dear God, is that lifelong learning requires fewer years than when I was in my twenties.

I've heard it said that if people do one thing each day that needs doing they'll always be caught up on chores. I don't think so. As soon as I cross one job off my list, another takes its place. Maybe that's because I forget what I did so I have to start over.

I don't have a problem forgiving people for what they've done to me, Lord. That's one advantage of becoming forgetful.

When I need a good laugh instead of a good cry, dear Father in heaven, I turn on the cartoon channel. After watching for a while I feel a lot better about some of the silly stunts I pull. Those cartoon characters do the same things, and they're not even seniors!

If there is a reason for every season under the sun, as Ecclesiastes, chapter 3, says, then I guess there's a reason for all these senior moments. Show me the positives, Lord, and help me handle my forgetful times with grace and wit.

I can't lose if I smile and shake someone's hand. Being kind is always appropriate and appreciated. Help make those moments a priority, Lord.

Every time I read I'm facing a book, right, Lord? So what's so special about Facebook?

Some people say it's not safe for older people to be alone too much. They might fall and break a hip, or burn down the house, or flood the yard, or run the car into a lamppost. But, Lord, I disagree. Time alone gives us golden opportunities to focus on you and read your Word.

I left the water running in the garden. Thank you, Lord, for bringing it to my attention in the nick of time or we'd have had a flood!

What a blessing, dear God, to know you are with me 24/7—especially when I take a pain pill when I mean to take a vitamin.

I'm continually praying about where I left my glasses. Today they're where they belong—in front of my eyes. Thank you, God.

I'm becoming notorious for burning our morning toast and letting our coffee go cold because I talk too much. Lord, help me stay on task.

God, can you imagine? I tried to light the fake logs in the fireplace. I'm so blessed to know you're looking out for my safety. Thank you.

Lord, what could be better than drinking a cup of tea with you in this sunset time of my life? Nothing!

Lord, thanks for holding me up a little longer, especially today when I blamed my husband for leaving the front door unlocked overnight and then realized it was my fault because I was the last one home. Thank you for giving me the courage to confess and ask for your forgiveness and my husband's.

God, thank you that I'm not paying attention to the fashion police anymore and can relax and enjoy wearing sneakers, jeans, and sweatshirts wherever I go.

Senior moments become points of humor as we age. Lord, help me look at them with gratitude because when I'm in a fix or a jam, I can turn to you in prayer and ask for help. And since you said you'll never leave me or forsake me, I know I can always rest in you. What great news!

365 Senior Moments You'd Rather Forget

We all experience them. You know—those momentary mental lapses that remind us we're only human. Humorist Karen O'Connor shares this great collection of senior moments to tickle your funny bone and let you know you're not alone. If you've ever...

- left the keys in the front door lock and gone to sleep feeling safe and secure

- purchased a book on improving memory but left it at the checkout counter

- dropped a boat anchor and then realized you forgot to tie it to the boat

welcome to the club! These true "senior moment" stories will help you remember that laughter makes every age a season to enjoy and treasure.

When God Answers Your Prayers

Yes, God is listening! Sharing inspiring stories, bestselling author Karen O'Connor encourages you to talk to God often and to patiently wait for his answers. Although God's timing may differ from yours, his responses and solutions are always perfect—even when they come just in the nick of time. Let these short devotions inspire you as they reveal how God has answered prayers like yours, including:

- restoring a soured friendship through grace and forgiveness
- blessing a struggling family when an anonymous donor sends furnace fuel
- strengthening a couple's faltering marriage when an unexpected circumstance brings them closer
- turning a job seeker's frustration to joy when a better position is offered

Whether praying is new to you or you pray every day, these upbeat stories will remind you that God loves you. He always sends his wonderful provision—sometimes in surprising ways and at unexpected times.

Grandma, You Rock!

Grandkids keep us young-at-heart, humble, and wide-awake!

Nothing beats being a grandparent—and these stories prove it! Grandma and bestselling author Karen O'Connor shares more than 80 true-life vignettes that highlight the delightful, humorous, and astounding ways grandchildren touch our hearts. Each tale celebrates the myriad blessings God gives us through these precious family members.

Every short story ends with an encouraging Scripture and a brief prayer asking God to help you make a positive difference in the lives of your grandchildren, who help you love and laugh in ways you never imagined.

As Karen says,

> *"What would our lives be like without sticky kisses, heavenly hugs, and hand-printed birthday notes?"*